Christmas 2009

D0667543

mc

# The Best of
## FAVORITE RECIPES FROM QUILTERS

# PIES

*Louise Stoltzfus*

## Good Books
Intercourse, PA 17534
Printed and bound in Hong Kong

Cover design and illustrations by Cheryl Benner
Design by Dawn J. Ranck

PIES: THE BEST OF FAVORITE RECIPES FROM QUILTERS
Copyright © 1994 by Good Books, Intercourse, Pennsylvania
17534
International Standard Book Number: 1-56148-115-7
Library of Congress Catalog Card Number: 94-14905

**Library of Congress Cataloging-in-Publication Data**

Pies / [compiled by] Louise Stoltzfus.
          p. cm. — (The Best of Favorite recipes from quilters)
      Includes index.
      ISBN 1-56148-115-7 : $7.95
      1. Pies.  I. Stoltzfus, Louise, 1952-  .  II. Series
TX773.P515    1994
641.8′652—dc20
                                                    94-14905
                                                       CIP

# INTRODUCTION

Amid the rush and haste of life, many people seek rest and quiet in community life. Quilters find community in common goals and activities. They talk of needles and thread, fabric and stitches, and bedcovers and pieces of art. They gather in homes, fabric shops, and convention centers to share their ideas and projects.

Many quilters are also homemakers. Some treat both cooking and quilting as high art forms. Others work hard to prepare varied and healthful meals for their busy families and quilt when they have free time.

From Sour Cream Apple Pie to Fresh Strawberry Pie to Shoofly Pie, these Pie recipes are both practical and delicious. Those who love to quilt and those who love to cook will share in the special vibrancy of this small collection.

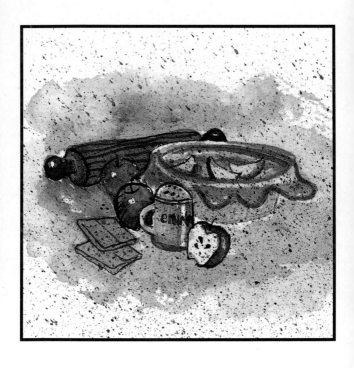

# FRENCH APPLE PIE

Barbara F. Shie, Colorado Springs, CO

*6-8 cooking apples*
*1 tsp. cinnamon*
*1 cup graham cracker crumbs*
*½ cup flour*
*1 cup sugar*
*½ tsp. ground nutmeg*
*¼ tsp. ground ginger*
*8 Tbsp. butter or margarine, melted*
*1 9" unbaked pie shell*

1. Peel, core and thinly slice apples.
2. Combine all dry ingredients.
3. Sprinkle 1 Tbsp. dry ingredients over bottom of deep-dish crust. Add layer of apple slices followed by layer of dry mixture. Continue alternating layers until apples are mounded in pie shell. Top with any remaining dry ingredients.
4. Carefully drizzle melted butter over all.
5. Bake at 350° for approximately 1 hour. Serve.

*Makes 1 deep-dish 9" pie*

# APPLESCOTCH MERINGUE PIE

LaVerne A. Olson, Willow Street, PA

### Filling
*1 cup brown sugar*
*1 cup water*
*1½ tsp. vinegar*
*6 large apples, pared and sliced*
*3 Tbsp. butter*
*4 Tbsp. flour*
*½ tsp. salt*
*1 9" baked pie shell*

### Meringue
*2 egg whites*
*4 Tbsp. sugar*
*1 tsp. vanilla*

1. Combine brown sugar, water and vinegar in a saucepan. Bring to a boil. Add apples and cook until tender. Remove apples from syrup and set aside.
2. Cream together butter and flour. Stir into hot syrup and cook until thickened and smooth, stirring constantly. Add salt and fold in apples. Cool. Turn into 9-inch baked pie shell.
3. To prepare meringue beat egg whites until stiff. Add sugar and vanilla and beat until just combined. Spread meringue over pie filling.
4. Bake at 350° for 9-10 minutes until meringue is lightly browned.

*Makes 1 9" pie*

# SOUR CREAM APPLE PIE

Lee Ann Hazlett, Freeport, IL

### *Filling*
*6-8 apples*
*1¼ cups sugar*
*2 heaping Tbsp. flour*
*2 tsp. vanilla*
*2 eggs*
*¼ tsp. salt*
*⅔ cup sour cream*
*½ tsp. cinnamon*
*1 9" unbaked pie shell*

### *Topping*
*½ cup sugar*
*⅓ cup flour*
*1 tsp. cinnamon*
*4 Tbsp. butter*
*½ cup chopped nuts*

1. Fill unbaked pie shell ¾ full with sliced apples.
2. Combine sugar, flour, vanilla, eggs, salt, sour cream and cinnamon and pour over apples.
3. Bake at 350° for 45-50 minutes.
4. To prepare topping combine all ingredients. Remove pie from oven and sprinkle topping ingredients over all. Return to oven and bake another 15 minutes.

*Makes 1 9" pie*

# Ambrosia Apple Pie

Jeannette R. Saunders, Albuquerque, NM

*1½ cups quick-cooking oats*
*1½ cups water*
*½ tsp. salt*
*1¾ cups sugar*
*4 Tbsp. flour*
*4 large, tart apples*
*¼ cup water*
*½ tsp. cinnamon*
*1 Tbsp. butter*
*1 9" unbaked pie shell*

1. In a saucepan cook oats, 1½ cups water and salt for 5 minutes. Press mixture through a sieve or run through food processor for several minutes. Reserve ½ cup of strained oat mixture.
2. Mix remaining oats with 1 cup sugar and flour. Pour into unbaked pie shell.
3. Pare and slice apples into a saucepan. Add ¼ cup water. Cover and cook apples over low heat for 10 minutes. Drain off all juice. Arrange apple slices over oatmeal mixture.
4. Combine ¾ cup sugar and cinnamon. Sprinkle over apples. Spread ½ cup strained oat mixture over top. Dot with butter.
5. Bake at 450° for 20 minutes or until done. Cool completely and serve with favorite cheese.

*Makes 1 9" pie*

# SWEDISH APPLE PIE

Charlotte Shaffer, Ephrata, PA

*2-3 cups sliced apples*
*1 tsp. nutmeg*
*1 tsp. cinnamon*
*½ tsp. sugar*
*1 cup sugar*
*1 cup flour*
*½ cup chopped nuts*
*8 Tbsp. butter, melted*
*1 egg*
*1 10" unbaked pastry shell*

1. Fill pastry shell ¾ full with sliced apples.
2. Combine nutmeg, cinnamon and ½ tsp. sugar and sprinkle over apples.
3. In a mixing bowl combine 1 cup sugar, flour, nuts, melted butter and egg. Spread mixture over apples.
4. Bake at 350° for 40-45 minutes.

*Makes 1 10" pie*

# NAKED APPLE PIE

Rosalie W. Keegan, Enfield, CT

*1 egg*
*½ cup brown sugar*
*½ cup white sugar*
*1 tsp. vanilla*
*Pinch salt*
*½ cup flour*
*1 tsp. baking powder*
*2 medium apples, peeled and sliced*
*½ cup chopped pecans*

1. Beat egg in medium bowl. Add sugars, vanilla, salt, flour and baking powder and mix well. Stir in apples and pecans.
2. Spread ingredients into greased 9-inch pie plate.
3. Bake at 350° for ½ hour. Serve with whipped cream or ice cream.

*Makes 1 9" pie*

---

My mother-in-law has made a practice of giving each of her grandchildren a quilt on their sixth birthday. She also presents each child with a memories scrapbook covering the events of the first six years of their lives. They anticipate this birthday for months and feel so special when it finally arrives.

Rebecca Meyer Korth, Wamego, KS

# RHUBARB APPLE PIE

Nancy George, De Pere, WI

*3½ cups diced, tart apples*
*2 cups diced rhubarb*
*1 cup sugar*
*¼ tsp. salt*
*½ tsp. cinnamon*
*3 Tbsp. minute tapioca*
*2 Tbsp. butter*
*Pastry for 2-crust pie*

1. Combine apples, rhubarb, sugar, salt, cinnamon and tapioca and mix well. Turn into pastry-lined 9-inch pie pan. Dot with butter. Cover with pastry top and seal edges.
2. Bake at 425° for 10-15 minutes. Reduce oven temperature to 375° and bake another 30-40 minutes.

*Makes 1 deep-dish 9" pie*

# SOUR CREAM RHUBARB PIE

Karen M. Rusten, Waseca, MN

*3 cups diced rhubarb*
*1 egg, slightly beaten*
*1½ cups sugar*
*Dash salt*
*3 Tbsp. tapioca*
*1 cup sour cream*
*1 9" unbaked pie shell*

1. Arrange rhubarb in pie shell.
2. Blend together egg, sugar, salt, tapioca and sour cream. Pour over rhubarb.
3. Bake at 450° for 15 minutes. Reduce oven temperature to 350° and bake 35-45 minutes longer or until filling has set.

*Makes 1 deep-dish 9" pie*

---

When our exchange student, Belen Pereira, prepared to return to her home in Argentina, she remarked that she would have two memories of me—my special bean salad recipe and my habit of cutting cloth into little pieces only to sew them back together again.

Shirley Norris, Walhounding, OH

# STRAWBERRY RHUBARB PIE

Marilyn Maurstad, Beatrice, NE

*2 cups diced rhubarb*
*2 cups sliced strawberries*
*1¼ cups sugar*
*4 Tbsp. minute tapioca*
*¼ tsp. salt*
*1 Tbsp. butter*
*Pastry for 2-crust pie*

1. Combine rhubarb and strawberries in large bowl.
2. Combine sugar, tapioca and salt in small bowl. Add to fruit and let stand while preparing pastry.
3. Spoon rhubarb mixture into pie shell. Dot with butter. Cover with top crust. Slit top and flute edges.
4. Bake at 400° for 40-45 minutes.

*Makes 1 9" pie*

# RHUBARB CUSTARD PIE

Silva Beachy, Millersburg, OH
Jacqueline E. Deininger, Bethlehem, PA
Cecilia Stevens, Pittsburgh, PA

*2 cups finely chopped rhubarb*
*1¼ cups white sugar*
*1 rounded Tbsp. flour*
*½ cup cream*
*2 eggs*
*½ cup water*
*½ tsp. nutmeg*
*1 9" unbaked pie shell*

1. Arrange rhubarb in unbaked pie shell.
2. Mix together sugar, flour, cream, eggs and water. Pour over rhubarb. Sprinkle with nutmeg.
3. Bake at 400° for 10 minutes. Reduce oven temperature to 325° and bake another 35-40 minutes or until set.

*Makes 1 9" pie*

# PINK LADY PIE

Mrs. Crist H. Yoder, Hutchinson, KS

*2 cups diced rhubarb*
*1 cup sugar*
*½ cup water*
*3-oz. pkg. strawberry gelatin*
*1 Tbsp. lemon juice*
*2 cups whipped topping*
*1 9" baked pie shell*

1. Cook rhubarb, sugar and water slowly until rhubarb is tender. Add dry gelatin and stir gently until dissolved. Let cool. Add lemon juice and cool to room temperature. Fold in whipped topping.
2. Spoon into baked pie shell and refrigerate to chill. Serve.

*Makes 1 9" pie*

A highlight of my young quilting years was being featured with my mother and grandmother as three generations of quilters at a quilt show in my home community of Freeman, SD. Though we now live 500 miles apart, my mother and I still frequently consult each other on quilting patterns and materials.

Lois Landis, Sterling, IL

# LETTIE'S PINEAPPLE PIE

Myrtle Mansfield, Alfred, ME

### Crust
2 cups graham cracker crumbs
½ cup sugar
8 Tbsp. margarine or butter

### Filling
2 small pkgs. instant vanilla pudding
20-oz. can crushed pineapple, undrained
1 pint sour cream

### Topping
½ pint whipping cream
1 tsp. vanilla

1. To prepare crust combine all ingredients and press into 9-inch pie pan.
2. Bake at 325° for 15 minutes. Cool.
3. To prepare filling combine all ingredients. Pour into cooled pie crust and refrigerate until filling sets.
4. To prepare topping combine cream and vanilla and whip until cream is spreadable. Immediately before serving, top filling with whipped cream.

*Makes 1 9" pie*

# PINEAPPLE CHEESE PIE

Maryalice DeLong, Elwood, IN

⅔ cup fine graham cracker crumbs
2 Tbsp. butter or margarine, softened
8-oz. pkg. lite cream cheese, softened
2 eggs or ½ cup egg substitute
¼ cup orange juice
¼ cup sugar
1 Tbsp. flour
1 Tbsp. vanilla
1 tsp. grated orange rind
Pinch salt (optional)
12-oz. can pineapple tidbits
1 tsp. unflavored gelatin

1. Combine graham cracker crumbs and butter. Mix well and press evenly into bottom of 9-inch pie pan.
2. Cream cream cheese. Add eggs and mix until smooth. Add orange juice, sugar, flour, vanilla, orange rind and salt. Mix until smooth. Pour into crumb crust.
3. Bake at 350° for 20-30 minutes or until filling is set. Chill.
4. To prepare a topping drain pineapple juice into a saucepan. Soften gelatin in juice and warm gently until it dissolves. Chill until mixture begins to thicken.
5. Arrange pineapple tidbits over baked pie filling. Pour gelatin mixture over all. Chill for 1 hour or until firm. Serve.

*Makes 1 9" pie*

# PEACH PIE

Anita Falk, Mountain Lake, MN

*6-8 fresh peaches, sliced*
*½ cup cream*
*1 heaping Tbsp. flour*
*1 cup sugar*
*Pinch salt*
*1 tsp. cinnamon*
*1 9" unbaked pie shell*

1. Arrange peach slices in pie shell.
2. Mix all remaining ingredients well and pour over peach slices.
3. Bake at 425° for 10 minutes. Reduce oven temperature to 375° and bake another 30-35 minutes.

*Makes 1 9" pie*

My mother often hosted quilting parties in the summertime. Two quilts would be set up in the front yard, and on the appointed day aunts, cousins and neighbors arrived for the quilting bee. We little girls were given the task of making lemonade to serve to the women. Our arms would be worn out from pounding enough lemons for several gallons of lemonade.

Kathryn M. Geissinger, Ephrata, PA

# ITALIAN PEACH PIE

Debbie Chisholm, Fallston, MD

### *Crust*
*8-oz. pkg. cream cheese*
*8 Tbsp. butter*
*½ tsp. salt*
*2 cups flour*

### *Filling*
*2 cups crushed vanilla wafers*
*8-10 fresh peaches*
*1½ cups sugar*
*¾ tsp. cinnamon*
*⅓ cup butter, melted*

1. Cream together cream cheese and butter. Add salt and work in flour. Divide dough and press into 2 9-inch pie pans.
2. Sprinkle with vanilla wafer crumbs.
3. Core, peel and slice peaches. Add sugar and cinnamon and mix well. Spoon over wafer crumbs in pie pans. Drizzle butter over peaches.
4. Bake at 350° for 45-60 minutes.

*Makes 2 9" pies*

# FRESH PEACH PIE

Trudi Cook, Newtown Square, PA

### *Crust*
*3 cups flour*
*1 cup cooking oil*
*1 tsp. salt*
*¼ cup sugar*
*¼ cup milk*

### *Filling*
*2 cups water*
*1 cup sugar*
*6 Tbsp. cornstarch*
*4 Tbsp. light corn syrup*
*6-oz. pkg. peach gelatin*
*10-12 fresh peaches*

1. To prepare crust combine all ingredients and mix well. Divide dough in half and press into 2 greased 9-inch square baking pans.
2. Bake at 400° for 10-15 minutes.
3. To prepare filling combine water, sugar, cornstarch and syrup in a saucepan. Bring to a boil and cook until thickened and clear, stirring constantly. Remove from heat and measure exactly 4 Tbsp. peach gelatin into mixture. Stir and cool slightly.
4. Core, peel and dice peaches. Fold into gelatin mixture. Divide mixture evenly between 2 baking dishes. Cool and serve.

*Makes 2 9" square pies*

# APRICOT PIE

Eleanor J. Ferreira, North Chelmsford, MA

*2 cups dried apricots*
*2 cups water*
*½ cup sugar*
*1½ Tbsp. cornstarch*
*Pinch salt*
*3 Tbsp. butter*
*Pastry for 2-crust pie*

1. In a saucepan bring apricots and water to a boil. Cook for 10 minutes. Add sugar and cook another 5 minutes. Drain, reserving 1 cup of juice. Set apricots aside.
2. Pour 1 cup reserved apricot juice into saucepan and add cornstarch. Add salt and cook until mixture thickens, stirring frequently.
3. Arrange drained apricots in unbaked pie shell. Pour in thickened apricot juice. Dot with butter.
4. Cover with top crust. Slit top and flute edges.
5. Bake at 425° for 30 minutes.

*Makes 1 9" pie*

# CRANBERRY PIE

Elizabeth Haderer, East Quogue, NY

*2 cups sliced cranberries*
*1 cup seedless raisins*
*2 Tbsp. flour*
*1 cup sugar*
*⅛ tsp. salt*
*½ cup water*
*Pastry for 2-crust pie*

1. Combine cranberries and raisins.
2. Combine flour, sugar and salt. Stir into cranberry and raisin mixture. Add water and mix well. Spoon into unbaked pie shell. Cover with top crust.
3. Bake at 425° for 10 minutes. Reduce oven temperature to 350° and bake another 25 minutes or until done.

*Makes 1 9" pie*

---

I'm still quite new at quilting, but last summer my mother remembered having some patches which had been made by my grandmother more than 50 years ago. She gave them to me and I created a full-size bedspread. When I gave the spread to my parents as a surprise, they were both speechless.

Kim Marlor, Owings Mills, MD

# FRESH STRAWBERRY PIE

Julie Lynch Arnsberger, Gaithersburg, MD
Cindy Cooksey, Irvine, CA

*6-oz. pkg. strawberry gelatin*
*1 cup sugar*
*1 Tbsp. cornstarch*
*2 cups boiling water*
*1 quart fresh strawberries*
*1 cup whipped topping*
*1 9" baked pie shell*

1. Combine gelatin, sugar and cornstarch in saucepan.
   Gradually add boiling water and stir to dissolve.
   Bring to a boil. Remove from heat and cool at least 5
   minutes.
2. Fold strawberries into gelatin mixture, reserving 5-6
   berries for garnish. Pour into baked pie shell.
3. Refrigerate at least 4 hours to chill. Immediately
   before serving, top with whipped topping and garnish
   with whole strawberries.

*Makes 1 9" pie*

# LEMON MERINGUE PIE

Blanche Cahill, Willow Grove, PA

### *Filling*
*1½ cups sugar*
*1½ cups water*
*¼ tsp. salt*
*½ cup cornstarch*
*⅓ cup water*
*4 egg yolks, slightly beaten*
*½ cup lemon juice*
*3 Tbsp. butter*
*1 tsp. grated lemon rind*
*1 9" baked pie shell*

### *Meringue*
*4 egg whites*
*¼ tsp. salt*
*½ cup sugar*

1. Combine sugar, 1½ cups water and salt in a saucepan. Heat to boiling.
2. Mix cornstarch with ⅓ cup water to make smooth paste. Gradually pour into boiling sugar mixture, stirring constantly. Cook until thickened and clear. Remove from heat.
3. Combine egg yolks and lemon juice. Stir into thickened mixture. Return to heat and cook, stirring constantly until mixture comes to a boil. Stir in butter and lemon rind. Remove from heat, cover and cool to lukewarm.

4. To prepare meringue add salt to egg whites and beat until fluffy. Gradually add sugar, beating until glossy peaks form. Stir 2 rounded Tbsp. meringue into lemon filling.
5. Pour lemon filling into baked pie shell. Spoon remaining meringue over top, swirling into peaks.
6. Bake at 325° for about 15-20 minutes or until meringue is lightly browned. Cool 1 hour before serving.

*Makes 1 9" pie*

When my husband interrupted his farming career to return to the classroom in the middle of a school year, our five-year-old son, who was accustomed to spending his days with Daddy, did not know quite what to do with me. One day I suggested we make a quilt. He happily ran from the ironing board to the sewing machine, bringing me tools and patches and making appropriate remarks about how the quilt was turning out. Patching redeemed that bleak January and February and we went on to find a reasonable daily rhythm. Today he still picks out his favorite patches from the quilt which is now used on his sister's bed.

Elaine W. Good, Lititz, PA

# CREAMY CHERRY PIE

Brenda Stanfield, Costa Mesa, CA

*16-oz. can cherry pie filling*
*½ tsp. almond extract*
*8-oz. pkg. cream cheese, softened*
*1 cup powdered sugar*
*1 cup heavy whipping cream*
*1 9" baked graham cracker crust*

1. Combine pie filling and almond extract and set aside.
2. Cream together cream cheese and powdered sugar.
3. Whip cream. Fold into cream cheese mixture. Spoon into graham cracker crust. Spread cherry pie filling over all.
4. Chill and serve.

*Makes 1 9" pie*

---

During the spring of 1991 I quilted a Double Irish Chain with appliqued hearts for my daughter's bed. She was four years old and I lost count of the times she asked, "Is it finished yet?"

To my surprise she insited on taking the finished quilt to her preschool for "Show and Tell." We managed to fold that full-size quilt into a 17" x 21" "Show and Tell" bag. Her peers rewared her with lots of oohs and aahs.

Judy Steiner Buller, Beatrice, NE

# FROZEN SUMMER PIE

Pat Higgins, Norman, OK

*6-oz. can frozen orange juice concentrate*
*1 pint vanilla ice cream, softened*
*3½ cups whipped topping*
*1 9" graham cracker pie shell*

1. In large bowl beat orange juice concentrate for 30 seconds. Blend in ice cream. Fold in whipped topping. If necessary, freeze until mixture will mound.
2. Spoon into prepared graham cracker crust. Freeze until firm, at least 4 hours.
3. Let stand at room temperature for 10 minutes before serving.

*Makes 1 9" pie*

My young daughter, upon overhearing a comment about the number of quilts I produce, remarked wtih great sadness, "My mother used to cook."

Paula Lederkramer, Levittown, NY

# RASPBERRY PARFAIT PIE

Susan L. Schwarz, North Bethesda, MD

*10-oz. pkg. frozen raspberries*
*3-oz. pkg. raspberry gelatin*
*1 pint vanilla ice cream*
*1 cup heavy cream*
*1 9" graham cracker pie shell*

1. Thaw and drain juice from raspberries. Add hot water to make 1½ cups liquid. Set raspberries aside.
2. Dissolve gelatin in 1½ cups hot raspberry liquid. Stir well.
3. While still hot, add ice cream, stirring until ice cream melts.
4. Refrigerate until partially set. Fold in raspberries. Pour filling into pie shell. Refrigerate to chill thoroughly.
5. Immediately before serving, whip cream.
6. Top raspberry filling with whipped cream and serve.

*Makes 1 9" pie*

# MISS JENNIE'S PUMPKIN PIE

Barbara G. Mann, Beatrice, NE

*1 cup sugar*
*1 tsp. cinnamon*
*½ tsp. ginger*
*½ tsp. nutmeg*
*½ tsp. salt*
*2 Tbsp. flour*
*1 cup pumpkin*
*1 cup evaporated milk*
*2 eggs, well beaten*
*1 Tbsp. margarine, melted*
*1 8" unbaked pie shell*

1. Combine sugar, spices and flour. Add all other ingredients and beat until smooth. Pour into unbaked pie shell.
2. Bake at 400° for 15 minutes. Reduce oven temperature to 350° and bake another 45 minutes or until knife blade comes out clean when inserted in center of pie.

*Makes 1 8" pie*

# SPICY PUMPKIN PIE

Vicky Jo Bogart, Fargo, ND

*2 eggs, slightly beaten*
*16-oz. can pumpkin*
*½ cup real maple syrup*
*½ tsp. salt*
*1-1½ tsp. cinnamon*
*¾ tsp. nutmeg*
*½ tsp. ginger*
*¼-½ tsp. ground cloves*
*1 tsp. pure vanilla*
*1 cup soy milk*
*1 9" unbaked pie shell*

1. In a large bowl combine all ingredients in the order listed except pie shell. Mix well and pour into unbaked pie shell.
2. Bake at 425° for 15 minutes. Reduce oven temperature to 350° and bake another 40-50 minutes or until knife inserted in center comes out clean.

*Makes 1 9" pie*

**Note:** *This recipe was created to accommodate a low sugar, dairy-free diet.*

# ZUCCHINI PIE

Mary Helen Wade, Sterling, IL

*4 cups grated zucchini*
*¾ cup white sugar*
*2 Tbsp. lemon juice*
*1 tsp. cinnamon*
*1 cup flour*
*½ cup brown sugar*
*8 Tbsp. butter or margarine*
*1 9" unbaked pie shell*

1. Combine zucchini, white sugar, lemon juice and cinnamon. Spoon into unbaked pie shell.
2. Combine flour, brown sugar and butter and mix until creamy. (Add more butter if needed.) Spread creamed mixture over zucchini mixture.
3. Bake at 400° for 1 hour.

*Makes 1 9" pie*

# SWEET POTATO PIE

Mrs. Clarence E. Mitchell, Frederick, MD

*8 large sweet potatoes*
*1½ cups sugar*
*3 cups milk*
*2 tsp. nutmeg*
*1½ tsp. lemon extract*
*6 eggs*
*12 Tbsp. butter*
*3 9" unbaked pie shells*

1. Boil sweet potatoes in jackets until tender. Peel and mash.
2. Add all remaining ingredients and mix well. Pour into unbaked pie shells.
3. Bake at 450° for 15 minutes. Reduce oven temperature to 350° and bake another 45 minutes.

*Makes 3 9" pies*

# GERMAN SWEET CHOCOLATE PIE

Elaine Patton, West Middletown, PA

*4-oz. pkg. German sweet chocolate*
*¼ cup butter*
*12-oz. can evaporated milk*
*1¼ cups sugar*
*3 Tbsp. cornstarch*
*⅛ tsp. salt*
*2 eggs*
*1 tsp. vanilla*
*⅓ cup coconut*
*½ cup chopped pecans*
*1 9" unbaked pie shell*

1. In a saucepan melt chocolate with butter over low heat, stirring until blended. Remove from heat and gradually blend in milk.
2. Combine sugar, cornstarch and salt in a bowl. Beat in eggs and vanilla. Gradually blend in chocolate mixture.
3. Pour filling into unbaked pie shell. Sprinkle with coconut and pecans.
4. Bake at 375° for 45 minutes or until browned and puffed.

*Makes 1 9" pie*

# FUDGE PIE

Violette Denney, Carrollton, GA

*8 Tbsp. margarine*
*2 squares unsweetened chocolate*
*½ cup flour*
*1 cup sugar*
*Dash salt*
*3 eggs, beaten*
*1 cup chopped nuts (optional)*

1. In double boiler melt together margarine and chocolate.
2. In a bowl combine flour, sugar, salt and eggs. Mix well. Add chocolate mixture and mix well. If desired, fold in nuts.
3. Pour into greased 9-inch pie plate.
4. Bake at 350° for 25-30 minutes.

*Makes 1 9" pie*

# CHOCOLATE PRUNE PIE

Lois Landis, Sterling, IL

*24 large marshmallows*
*½ cup milk*
*1 cup cooked prunes, chopped*
*¾ cup whipping cream*
*2 ozs. semi-sweet chocolate, shaved*
*1 9" baked pie shell*

1. In a saucepan heat milk and marshmallows until melted. Cool and fold in chopped prunes.
2. Whip cream into soft peaks. Reserve ½ cup whipped cream and 2 Tbsp. chocolate shavings. Fold remaining whipped cream and chocolate into marshmallow mix. Pour into baked pie shell.
3. Chill in refrigerator. Top with reserved whipped cream and chocolate shavings and serve.

*Makes 1 9" pie*

# WALNUT PIE

JoAnn Pelletier, Longmeadow, MA
Katie's Quilts, Millersburg, OH

*4 Tbsp. butter or margarine, melted*
*½ cup white sugar*
*½ cup brown sugar*
*¼ tsp. salt*
*3 eggs, beaten*
*½ cup evaporated milk*
*¼ cup light corn syrup*
*½ tsp. vanilla*
*1 cup chopped walnuts*
*1 9" unbaked pie shell*

1. Combine butter, sugars and salt. Add eggs and mix well. Stir in milk, corn syrup, vanilla and walnuts. Pour into pie shell.
2. Bake at 400° for 25-30 minutes or until knife inserted in center comes out clean.

*Makes 1 9" pie*

# PECAN PIE

Alana Robbins, Los Lunas, NM
Esther L. Lantz, Leola, PA
Marjorie Miller, Partridge, KS

*1 cup pecans*
*3 large eggs*
*¾ cup light or dark corn syrup*
*1 cup sugar or less*
*¼ cup butter or margarine, melted*
*1 tsp. vanilla*
*¼ tsp. salt*
*1 9" unbaked pie shell*

1. Arrange pecans evenly in unbaked pie shell.
2. Combine all remaining ingredients and mix well. Pour over pecans.
3. Bake at 350° for 40-50 minutes.

*Makes 1 9" pie*

When my husband and I moved off our farm, I began making quilts for our six grandchildren. In September of 1981 we bought a frame, and I began making quilts to sell. As of April 1992 I am working on my 112th quilt.

Evelyn Becker, Paradise, PA

# GRAPENUT PIE

Phebe Hershberger, Goshen, IN

*½ cup grapenuts*
*½ cup warm water*
*3 eggs, well beaten*
*¾ cup sugar*
*1 cup dark corn syrup*
*Pinch salt*
*1 tsp. vanilla*
*3 Tbsp. butter, melted*
*1 9" unbaked pie shell*

1. Combine grapenuts and warm water. Let stand until water is absorbed.
2. Combine beaten eggs with all other ingredients except pie shell. Fold in grapenuts. Spoon into pie shell.
3. Bake at 350° for 50 minutes.

*Makes 1 9" pie*

# OUT OF THIS WORLD PIE

Sara M. Miller, Kalona, IA

*8 Tbsp. butter*
*1 cup sugar*
*3 eggs*
*¼ tsp. salt*
*½ tsp. vanilla*
*1 cup chopped nuts*
*1 cup raisins*
*1 9" unbaked pie shell*

1. Cream together butter and sugar. Add eggs, salt and vanilla and beat well. Stir in nuts and raisins. Spoon into unbaked pie shell.
2. Bake at 350° for 40-60 minutes or until browned on top.

*Makes 1 9" pie*

My mother-in-law, Catherine Seeley, taught me how to quilt many years ago. On our trips to Ithaca, NY she would reminisce about her family while we sat around the quilt talking and drinking tea. I learned so much about my husband and his family during those special times.

Sue Seeley, Black Forest, CO

# RAISIN CRUMB PIE

Minnie A. Stoltzfus, Lancaster, PA

*1 lb. raisins*
*Water to cover*
*¾ cup sugar*
*1 Tbsp. flour or cornstarch*
*2 cups flour*
*1 cup sugar*
*½ cup shortening*
*2 tsp. baking powder*
*2 eggs, beaten*
*1 cup milk*
*3 9" unbaked pie shells*

1. In a saucepan combine raisins, water to cover and ¾ cup sugar. Bring to a boil and boil slowly for 20 minutes. Add 1 Tbsp. flour to thicken. Stir well and set aside.
2. Mix together 2 cups flour, 1 cup sugar, shortening and baking powder until crumbly. Reserve ¾ cup crumbs.
3. To remaining crumbs add eggs and milk and mix well.
4. Divide raisin mixture evenly in pie shells. Spoon batter evenly over raisins. Top with reserved crumbs.
5. Bake at 350° for 40-45 minutes or until knife inserted in center comes out clean.

*Makes 3 9" pies*

# TOASTED COCONUT CREAM PIE

Frances Musser, Newmanstown, PA

*3-oz. pkg. instant vanilla pudding*
*8-oz. pkg. cream cheese, softened*
*½ cup powdered sugar*
*½ tsp. coconut flavoring*
*8-oz. container whipped topping*
*⅔ cup toasted coconut*
*1 10" baked pie shell*

1. Prepare pudding according to package directions.
2. Combine cream cheese and powdered sugar and beat until smooth. Add flavoring, whipped topping and pudding and mix well. Pour into baked pie shell.
3. To prepare toasted coconut spread in baking pan. Place under broiler for about 2 minutes. Watch carefully as this burns easily. Chill toasted coconut.
4. Spread coconut over pudding mixture and serve.

*Makes 1 10" pie*

# COCONUT CUSTARD BLENDER PIE

Mary Esther Yoder, Partridge, KS
Elsie Schlabach, Millersburg, OH
Sara Wolf, Washington, PA

*4 eggs*
*2 cups milk*
*½ cup flour*
*1 tsp. vanilla*
*1 cup sugar*
*6 Tbsp. butter*
*1 cup coconut*

1. Blend all ingredients together on high speed in blender for 10 seconds.
2. Pour into greased and floured 10-inch pie pan.
3. Bake at 350° for 1 hour.

*Makes 1 10" pie*

# CUSTARD PIE

Amanda Schlabach, Millersburg, OH

*3 eggs*
*½ cup white sugar*
*⅛ tsp. salt*
*2 cups scalded milk*
*2 tsp. vanilla*
*1 Tbsp. butter, melted*
*⅛ tsp. nutmeg*
*1 9" unbaked pie shell*

1. Beat eggs until light and foamy. Add sugar and salt and blend well. Add the scalded milk and vanilla.
2. Brush unbaked pie shell with melted butter. Pour custard into shell. Sprinkle lightly with nutmeg.
3. Bake at 450° for 10 minutes. Reduce oven temperature to 325° and bake another 25-30 minutes.

*Makes 1 9" pie*

My son Andy is a Miami Dolphins football fan. When I went to purchase fabric for a Bow Tie quilt I planned to make for him, the sales people at the store questioned my strange color choices—orange, white and aqua. My son is now 25 and quite proud of his Dolphins Bow Tie quilt.

Abbie Christie, Berkeley Heights, NJ

# CARAMEL WHIPPED CREAM PIE

Margaret Jarrett, Anderson, IN

*1 cup light brown sugar*
*7 Tbsp. flour*
*1 Tbsp. cornstarch*
*¼ tsp. salt*
*2 eggs, beaten*
*2 cups milk*
*2 Tbsp. butter*
*1 tsp. vanilla*
*2 pints whipping cream*
*1 Heath Bar, crushed*
*1 9" baked pie shell*

1. Combine sugar, flour, cornstarch and salt in a saucepan.
2. In a bowl combine beaten eggs and milk. Add to dry ingredients and cook until thickened, stirring constantly.
3. Remove from heat and add butter and vanilla, beating until smooth. Let cool.
4. Beat whipping cream until peaks form. Stir ⅔ of whipped cream into cooled mixture. Pour into baked pie shell. Spread remaining cream over pie. Sprinkle crushed Heath Bar over top and refrigerate. (This pie should be prepared a day in advance.)

*Makes 1 9" pie*

# SOUR CREAM PIE

Marjorie L. Benson, Yates City, IL

### *Pie*
1½ cups thick sour cream
1 cup powdered sugar
2 Tbsp. flour
2 egg yolks, well beaten
1 tsp. vanilla
½ cup seeded raisins
½ cup chopped nuts
1 9" baked pie shell

### *Meringue*
1 Tbsp. cornstarch
2 Tbsp. cold water
½ cup boiling water
3 egg whites
6 Tbsp. white sugar
Dash salt
1 tsp. vanilla

1. To prepare pie heat sour cream slowly. Add powdered sugar and continue heating slowly, stirring frequently.
2. Remove ½ cup creamed mixture and blend in flour. Pour back into creamed mixture and heat, stirring frequently. Add egg yolks and bring to a boil. Remove from heat and stir in vanilla, raisins and nuts. Cool.
3. Pour into 9-inch pie shell.
4. To prepare meringue blend cornstarch and cold water in a saucepan. Add boiling water and cook, stirring until thickened and clear. Let stand until completely cooled.
5. Using electric mixer beat egg whites until foamy. Gradually add sugar and beat until stiff, but not dry. Add salt and vanilla and continue beating on low speed. Gradually add cornstarch mixture and beat on high speed until well mixed.
6. Spread meringue over pie filling.
7. Bake at 350° for several minutes until meringue is golden brown.

*Makes 1 9" pie*

I come from a small farming and ranching community near Adrian, TX. Once or twice a month the women of the community got together for an all-day quilting bee. They sat around the quilt talking about their children, their relatives and the women who were not there on that particular day. We children loved the opportunity to run wild and free, playing games and climbing trees.

Linda Roberta Pond, Los Alamos, NM

# SHOOFLY PIE

Naomi Lapp, New Holland, PA

*1 cup flour*
*⅔ cup brown sugar*
*1 Tbsp. shortening*
*1 egg*
*¾ cup molasses*
*¾ cup boiling water*
*1 tsp. baking soda*

1. Mix together flour, brown sugar and shortening until crumbly. Reserve ½ cup crumbs. Arrange remaining crumbs across bottom of greased 9-inch pie pan.
2. In a bowl combine egg, molasses, boiling water and baking soda. Mix well and pour into pie pan. Cover with remaining crumbs.
3. Bake at 350° for 30 minutes.

*Makes 1 9" pie*

# CHEESECAKE PIE

Joy Moir, Holtsville, NY

*8-oz. pkg. cream cheese*
*½ cup sugar*
*2 eggs*
*1 cup sour cream*
*½ tsp. vanilla*
*1 9" unbaked graham cracker crust*

1. Cream together cream cheese and sugar. Add eggs, sour cream and vanilla. Spoon into graham cracker crust.
2. Bake at 350° for 40 minutes. Chill completely before serving.

*Makes 1 9" pie*

---

I discovered the world of quilts when my husband and I visited Lancaster County, PA on our honeymoon in 1977. After a long search we bought a Bridal Wreath quilt from an Old Order Mennonite woman. Fourteen years later we returned to this woman's shop and found it was now operated by her daughter. The daughter pointed out a Log Cabin quilt as the last one her mother had made. My husband gave me the Log Cabin quilt for our fourteenth wedding anniversary.

Debra M. Zeida, Waquoit, MA

# BLUE RIBBON PIE CRUST

Sandy Brown, Connersville, IN

*5 cups all-purpose flour*
*1¼ tsp. salt*
*1 tsp. baking powder*
*2½ cups shortening*
*1 tsp. vinegar*
*1 egg*

1. Combine flour, salt and baking powder. Cut in shortening until mixture has cornmeal texture.
2. In a 1-cup measure beat together vinegar and egg. Fill to 1 cup with cold water. Pour into flour mixture and work to mix. (Dough will be soft and sticky.)
3. Divide dough into 5 parts and roll out to ⅛-inch thickness. Put into lightly floured pie pans.
4. For pies requiring baked pie shells, press a piece of aluminum foil against the pie shell in pan.
5. Bake at 425° for 6 minutes. Remove aluminum foil and bake another 12 minutes. Cool completely.

*Makes 5 9" pie crusts*

***Variation:*** *After dividing dough into 5 parts, wrap each ball separately in wax paper or plastic wrap and chill until ready to use. This recipe keeps 3-4 days in refrigerator and also freezes well. When ready to use, simply thaw and roll out, continuing with step 3.*

Jean H. Robinson, Cinnaminson, NJ

# INDEX